Big dedication

This book is dedicated to my papa (grandpa), who always supported me—even when we were apart. Though distance kept us from being together, you always called to check in, and when we did see each other, you gave me some of the best memories. One moment I'll never forget is how proud you were when I was on Nickelodeon. If you could have seen me on Good Morning America, I think you would have been more amazed. Thank you, Papa, for giving me memories that will stay with me forever. This book is for you.

1950 - 2022

Table of contents

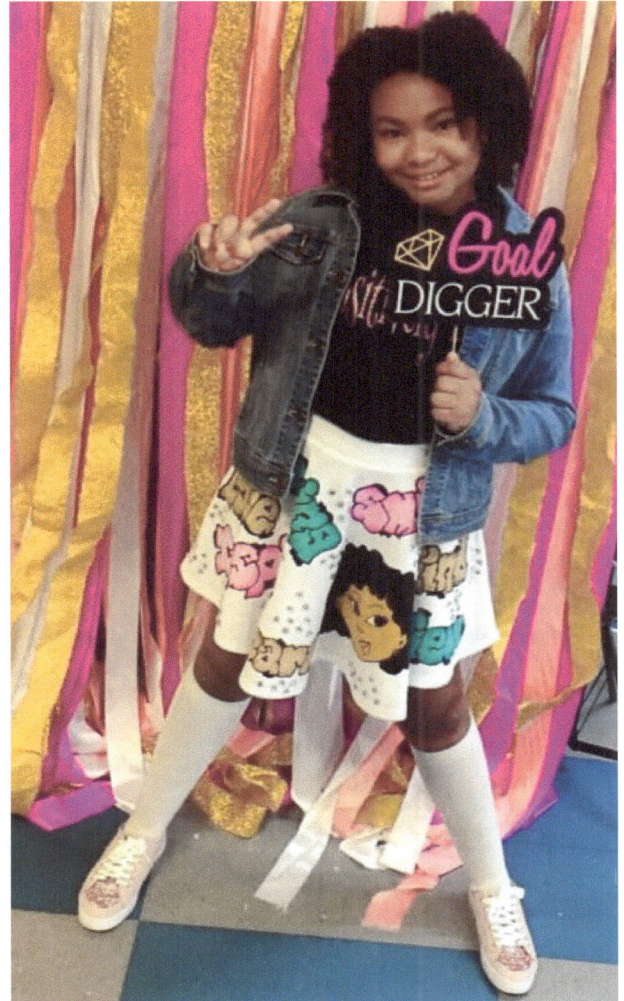

Introduction

Hello, and welcome to my story! My name is Lena Ford. I'm fifteen years old as I write this book, and by the time you'd be reading it, I'll be sixteen. I'm from Atlanta, Georgia, and I'm a youth entrepreneur, philanthropist, and author. I've been featured on Good Morning America, Nickelodeon, and more, all before turning sixteen!

As exciting as those moments are, what matters most is what I've learned along the way, and how you can apply those lessons to your own life.

I wrote this book to inspire at least one young person—whether kid or teen—to believe they can do anything they set their mind to, no matter their age. My journey began at seven years old, when I started collecting and donating art supplies to kids in foster care and shelters. That passion was inspired by someone very special: my great-grandmother, whom I call Granny. (You'll hear more about her later!)

In these chapters, you'll learn how I got started, what my life was like growing up, and the highs and lows of being a youth entrepreneur. You'll also find tips on how to begin chasing your own dreams.

If there's one thing I want you to take away from this book, it's this: Never let what others think stop you from becoming your best self.

Chapter One

The Spark Inside Me

Chapter one : The Spark Inside Me

Growing up between Marietta, Kennesaw, and Atlanta was a unique and special experience. I was raised by both of my parents, but I spent most of my time with my Granny, who shaped so much of who I am today. One of my earliest and favorite memories was visiting Brunswick, Georgia, where my Granny was from. I remember being about four or five years old, going to the beach with her and my mom. I cried when it was time to leave because I didn't want the fun to end. For years afterward, my clothes, bags, and shoes carried the scent of the sand, and I loved it. Every time I catch that smell even now, I'm reminded of those happy times with my family. Another memory that stands out is returning from Brunswick and dropping my Oma (grandma) off at her job. I cried so much that day, and everyone had to reassure me it would be okay. That moment showed just how much of a "family girl" I've always been. I also remember visiting family in Mississippi. We would sit outside while the adults cooked crawfish, and I played with my younger cousins. The younger me was a loving, caring, silly, and creative little girl who always wanted to be close to her family. You would often find me coloring, drawing, or painting. I loved sketching "portraits" of family members and proudly gifting the finished drawings to them. I was also a child model, which some people think negatively about, but for me it was one of the best experiences of my childhood. I made friends I still have to this day. Getting on stage, showing off creative outfits, and seeing the smiles and cheers from my family and the crowd always made me feel special.

Chapter one : The Spark Inside Me

But more than anything, I loved being around my Granny. Her home, her presence, and even the scents that lingered around her made me feel most like myself. She was one of my greatest inspirations. At just seven years old, she inspired me to launch my first initiative: collecting and donating art supplies for children in foster care and shelters. Granny always gave back, even when she didn't have much to give. Watching her find something, anything, to share with others filled my heart with joy. I wanted others to feel the same love she gave me. Granny was also the glue that held our family together. We celebrated every holiday with her. I remember packing my bag to take to my auntie's house just so that Granny could take me home with her after the party. Of course, I can't forget the contributions of my mom, dad, and the rest of my family. They always saw the best in me, teaching me lessons about leadership, bravery, kindness, and hard work. Looking back, I realize that my fun, silly, and creative younger self has shaped a lot of who I am today. She taught me not to care about other people's judgments, to do what makes me happy, and to remember that in the long run, what truly matters is living authentically and joyfully.

KIDS **BOOST**

Date 12/16/17

Pay to the order of CCYA & Kids Boost $ 461.00

Four hundred sixty-one /100 Dollars

fr. Lena's Paris in Pink Party

Lena Ford
Authorized Signature

Chapter two : Arting4You -- My First Mission

As I've mentioned before, my Granny always tried to give, even when she didn't have much to offer. That inspired me to start my very first initiative, Arting4You, where I collected and donated art supplies to children in foster homes and shelters. I was only seven years old when I began! It just goes to show that anything is possible if you set your mind to it. I've always loved art because it helps me express my emotions. Drawing and creating gave me a safe, positive way to let my feelings out, and I wanted other kids to have that same outlet. When I told my mom I wanted to donate art supplies, she encouraged me right away. She helped me buy materials and asked close family members to contribute. Soon, my school heard about what I was doing, and teachers even began donating extra supplies. It might sound like everything came together easily, but it wasn't that simple. The biggest challenge was finding places willing to accept donations. My mom and I searched everywhere, but it was surprisingly hard to get organizations to agree. That's when my mom connected me with an amazing group called Kids Boost. They helped us partner with another organization, CCYA (Center for Children & Young Adults), where I made my very first donation in 2017.

Chapter two : Arting4You – My First Mission

The joy I felt that day is hard to put into words. Knowing that something I started could help other kids was one of the most powerful feelings I've ever had. After that, I knew I didn't want to stop. Arting4You began to grow because of that one moment.

Even though I was so young, I realized it didn't matter, I could still make a difference. Getting the word out was tough, and I was still relying heavily on donations from my parents and close family. But once they saw how serious I was, my mom suggested something new: "What if you started a business to help fund this?"

At that moment, the idea of becoming a young entrepreneur was planted in my heart. But the question was, what kind of business could a nine-year-old start?

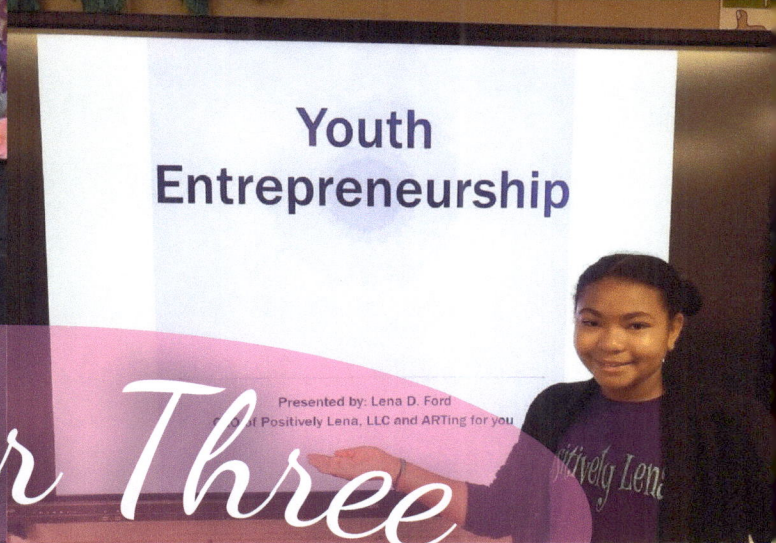

Chapter Three

Starting Positively Lena

Youth Entrepreneurship

Presented by: Lena D. Ford
Chief of Positively Lena, LLC and ARTing for you

Chapter Three: Starting Positively Lena

Positively Lena—that's the business I started at just nine years old. At first, it was a way to help fund Arting4You, but it quickly became something even bigger. I kept seeing stories about teenagers struggling with mental health, and the suicide rates were especially troubling. I wanted to create something that could serve as a reminder to keep going, no matter what.

Since I loved art, crafts, writing, and fashion, I decided to make accessories, something people could carry with them as a daily reminder. I chose keychains because they're simple, affordable, and always with you on a backpack, purse, or keyring.

When I told my mom my idea, she loved it. In fact, she came up with the name.

"How about Positively Lena?" she asked.

"What does positive mean?" I asked.

"It means to always look for the good, even when things go bad."

"I like that word, Mommy. Let's do it!"

Even though I didn't come up with the name completely on my own, that moment taught me something important: I didn't have to do everything by myself. From that day forward, positivity became a word I carried with pride, and I've tried my best to reflect it in my life and decisions.

At first, my mom and I made resin keychains together. We wore masks and gloves for safety, and after a while we began ordering pre-made materials to help us keep up. Eventually, I was ready for my very first vendor event.

Chapter Three: Starting Positively Lena

Luckily, I wasn't going in blind. My mentor, Julia Davis, invited me to shadow her at events before I launched my own table. Julia had written multiple books, created programs for kids to promote self-esteem, and she dreamed of opening her own bookstore. Helping her, taught me how to run a vendor table, greet and interact with customers, as well as believe in myself.

My first event was a kids' vendor fair, and I loved it. I met other young entrepreneurs, and I was surrounded by support. My mentor Julia came with her mom, my best friend showed up with her family, and my "village" encouraged me every step of the way. I'll never forget when a woman came to my table, looked me in the eye, and said:

"Keep going no matter what obstacles come up. What you're doing is really needed."

That moment changed my life. I realized then that I couldn't stop and if I kept going, I really could change lives.

Of course, running a business while going to school wasn't always easy. My strategy was to separate my time: schoolwork came first, then business after homework. But soon after I launched, I faced two huge challenges: my Granny passed away, and then COVID-19 hit and shut everything down. As a ten-year-old, it was heartbreaking and overwhelming.

Chapter Three: Starting Positively Lena

Even during that time, despite the uncertainties that we all faced, I didn't stop giving. I ran my website, continued to promote my business on social media, and participated in a Christmas drive where I helped buy gifts for kids in need. Delivering those gifts and seeing how grateful the organizers were, reminded me that giving is at the heart of everything I do.

When it was time to begin middle school, I tried public school for a year, but I quickly realized it wasn't the right environment for me. There was too much drama, too much stress, and even some teachers made me feel unwelcome. I didn't give up though, instead I wrote my parents a five–page persuasive essay on why I should be homeschooled. It worked, and I've been homeschooled for four years now.

Since then, I've thrived, skipping a grade, speaking to kids in schools, joining programs I wouldn't have found otherwise, and even going on Good Morning America.

That whole experience was unforgettable. At first, my mom thought the email from GMA was spam. But it turned out to be real. After a Zoom interview with a producer, they flew me to New York City. I stayed in a hotel in Times Square, met other incredible kids, got my makeup done, and appeared on live TV with Michael Strahan. On stage, I was surprised with a $10,000 donation from the hair care brand, Mielle Organics, to support my nonprofit, Kinship Family Initiative.

Moments like that remind me that everything I started with a single idea at age nine has grown into something so much bigger than I could have imagined.

First ever vending event

All the way to GMA

Chapter Four

More than just a business

Chapter Four: more than just a business

After writing my first book at twelve, I co-founded a nonprofit with my mom and her friends called the Kinship Family Initiative. Our mission is to support families in kinship care. This is when an adult relative raises a child who isn't their biological son or daughter. We organize drives, donation events, and kit-packing projects to help families with the resources they need. My mom's own story is what inspired this work. She was raised by her great-grandmother; my Granny, alongside her three brothers. She knew firsthand the challenges of kinship care: it's filled with love, but it can also be a struggle for everyone involved. We wanted to provide the kind of support that makes life a little easier for families going through this kind of situation.

That's why, whenever you purchase something from Positively Lena, please know that 30% of the proceeds go directly toward Kinship Family Initiative. Giving back has always been at the heart of what I do.

Now that you've learned my whole story, from a seven-year-old starting Arting4You, to creating Positively Lena, to co-founding a nonprofit. I've shown you that kids and teens really can make a difference. Now it's your turn. This chapter is about how you can take the first steps to bring your own ideas to life.

Senior speaking engagement

Step One: Getting Your Idea

Start with something you truly enjoy. Ask yourself, Can I see myself doing this long-term without getting bored? If the answer is yes, that's your starting point. But remember, it's okay to change your idea later. I began with keychains, bookmarks, and notebooks, but over time I discovered I also loved writing books, hosting events, and working directly with kids.

Step Two: Telling an Adult

Share your ideas with a trusted adult, parent, teacher, or mentor. You'll need their help, especially for the legal parts of starting a business. That includes registering your business or nonprofit and understanding taxes. (Pro tip: don't be afraid to use Google or even ChatGPT for research when you're stuck!)
I suggest using google or even ChatGPT for a more detailed breakdown.

Step Three: Creating a Plan

Write down your ideas in a document. Include your business name, the products or services you'll offer, pricing, whether you'll sell online or in person, and anything else you'll need to get started. Treat it as your blueprint

Step Four: Creating a Website
A website helps people learn who you are, what you sell, and why your business matters. Platforms like Shopify, Squarespace, or Wix make it easy to get started.

Step Five: Social Media
Set up social media accounts to promote your products and share your story. If you're under 18, ask a parent to help manage your account. Don't forget to link your website in your bio!

Step Six: Creating Products
Begin making your products. This might take trial and error, so don't get discouraged if the first version isn't perfect.

Step Seven: Setting Prices
Factor in the cost of materials, packaging, and your time. Make sure your price reflects the value of your product.

Step Eight: Finding Packaging
Pick packaging that fits your product—envelopes, labels, thank-you cards, or even wrapping paper and stickers. Remember: shipping costs money, so plan for it!

Step Nine: Sending Out Your Product

Once an order comes in, package it carefully and take it to your local post office. Keep your customer updated so they know when to expect their delivery.

Step Ten: Building Your Village

Encourage your first customers to leave reviews, share your business with friends, and follow you online. A strong support system will help you grow and stay motivated.

Starting something new can feel overwhelming, but step by step, you'll get there. If I could do it at seven, so can you.

YBK Day 2022

Planning your business part 1

Write down the products you would like to sell:

_____
- -
_____
- -
_____
- -
_____

Tell an adult: Who did you tell?

_____
- -
_____

Write down names for your future business!

-
-
-
-

-
-
-
-

Planning your business part 2

Business name:

_____

- -

_____

What product or service you will offer?

_____

- -

_____

- -

_____

- -

_____

Pricing:

- $
- $
- $
- $

- $
- $
- $
- $

Circle how you will sell

Online   In-person   Both

Chapter Five

Looking ahead

Chapter Five : Looking ahead

In the next four to five years, my dream is to become an elementary school teacher. I want to create a classroom where every child feels safe, supported, and inspired to dream big. I want my students to know from the moment they walk through the door that they are capable of amazing things, even when life feels hard.

One of my biggest long-term goals is to someday own a microschool or even a full school where students of all ages can learn in ways that fit their individual needs. I want each child to feel seen and valued, and to be given the space to grow to their full potential.

Reflecting on my journey so far, I've realized how much each part of my story has taught me:

· Arting4You taught me that no act of kindness is ever too small.

· Positively Lena taught me that spreading positivity matters, even when it's difficult. And if I fall short, that's okay because there's always another chance to do better.

· Giving back showed me that while I may have what I need to survive, others don't always have that luxury. If I can be a blessing to someone else, I must act.

· Growing up has taught me that life is always changing, sometimes because of my choices, sometimes because of the choices of others. But no matter what, I can find peace in being true to myself.

To anyone reading this, whether you're a kid, a teen, or an adult, my advice is simple: dream big, but don't stop at dreaming. Thinking and wishing will only take you so far. Action is what brings those dreams to life.

Never let what others think of you stop you from being your best self. And if no one has told you today: I love the person you are.

ilovemebookseries

Special thank you's

To those who made this journey special

Special Thank you's

Dear Mom, I thank you for being the best mom, co—founder, and business partner a girl can have. Thank you for being there off screen and on screen when it's needed most without you being here. I wouldn't have gotten to where I am today or even writing this book. I love YOU.

Dear Dad, I thank you for being the best dad I could ever ask for on the planet. From always being there when I need it most in serious times to being a person I can joke and be silly around even when mom looks at us like we're crazy. I appreciate you and all that you do even if I don't tell you all the time. I love YOU.

Dear family, Yes, family, on all sides, not just one. Thank you ALL for supporting me the day I entered this world, always loving me and caring for me from near by or faraway. I thank you all for being there with me no matter what! I love YOU ALL.

Me and my granny

Special Thank you's

Dear Ms. Julia, I thank you for being one of the very first ones to start me with this journey of becoming PositivelyLena. Meeting you at the age of seven has opened up more doors than I could have ever imagined myself in. I love YOU.

Dear Ms. Pearl, I thank you for being an excellent model coach at the age of six but even as years passed and I model less to no longer modeling you're still always there supporting me and including me. I love YOU.

Dear Ms. Ni'Cola, I thank you for being an amazing mentor I know I can always count on even in the worst of situations. Without GirlsWhoBrunch I wouldn't know some of the girls I know today. I love YOU.

Dear Mrs. Arriel, I thank you for being an excellent business mentor from opening up my door to helping me write my first ever book at the age of 12 to now being in my next book at the age of 15 is something I find crazy! Thank you for sticking with me through all these years. I love YOU.

Special Thank you's

Dear Ms. Sheva, I thank you for also sticking with me through all these years supporting me and teaching me all kinds of things from writing to entrepreneurship. You've done it all. And let me not forget having Ziggy and Tootie who I can always count on to be at almost every Kidpreneur event! I love YOU.

Dear Mrs. Tamika, I thank you for opening this door for me to write and publish my second book but also making my upperclass years in highschool a breeze which I really appreciate when everything is so difficult to understand and keep track with. Thank you for creating The Empress and Pearls. I love YOU.

To My Supporters and Customers: Thank you for making this journey possible. Without you, I don't know how far I would have come.

I love you ALL!

Follow me and stay connected

- ⓕ Facebook – @Positivelylena
- ⓞ Business Instagram – @PositivelyLena
- ⓞ Let's get connected Instagram – @Ms.Lena.Danielle
- ♪ TikTok – @PositivelyLena
- 🌐 Website – www.Positivelylena.com

Want to watch my GMA interview? search:

"Lena Ford GMA" if that doesn't work try "Young woman helps kids in foster care system GMA"

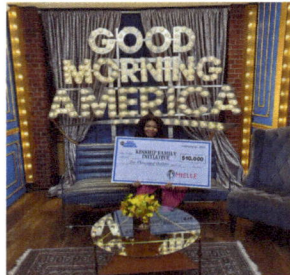

Want to watch my Ted Talk? search:

"Lena Ford Ted Talk" if that doesn't work try "Advice for Becoming a Young Entrepreneur...Right Now | Lena Ford | Être TED-Ed Club"